Family Feelings

by Tomás Gonzales

NATIONAL GEOGRAPHIC   **Hampton-Brown**

National Geographic and the Yellow Border are registered trademarks of the National Geographic Society.

National Geographic School Publishing
Hampton-Brown
www.NGSP.com

Printed in the USA.
RR Donnelley, Johnson City, TN

ISBN: 978-0-7362-7986-4

10 11 12 13 14 15 16 17 18 19   10 9 8 7 6 5 4 3 2

Acknowledgments and credits continue on the inside back cover.

She is happy.

He is excited.

She is surprised.

This family is happy together!